Junior World Explorers

Marco Polo

by Charles P. Graves
illustrated by Ray Keane

Chelsea Juniors
A division of Chelsea House Publishers
New York ■ Philadelphia

THE ASTROLABE, an instrument developed by the Greeks, is the symbol for JUNIOR WORLD EXPLORERS. At the time of Columbus, sailors used the astrolabe to chart a ship's course. The arm across the circle could be moved to line up with the sun or a star. Using the number indicated by the pointer, a sailor could tell his approximate location on the sea. Although the astrolabe was not completely accurate, it helped many early explorers in their efforts to conquer the unknown.

To those 20th-century Polos, Aunt Louise and Uncle Victor

Cover Illustration: Danny O'Leary

First Chelsea House edition 1991

5 7 9 8 6

ISBN   0-7910-1505-X

Contents

1

A Short Geography Lesson

Marco Polo was lying on his back beside a canal in Venice. His younger brother, Maffeo, was lying next to him. The boys were looking up at the stars.

"Maffeo," Marco said, "maybe Father is looking at the same stars right now."

"I wish he would come home," Maffeo said.

"He will some day," Marco promised. "I'm sure of that."

"How long has he been gone now?" Maffeo asked. The younger boy had been very little when his father went away. He could not even remember him.

Marco thought for a moment. "Father left in 1260 and it is 1264 now. Can't you figure that out?"

"That's easy," Maffeo answered. "Let's see, 1264 minus 1260. That leaves four. So Father has been gone for four years."

"You're getting good at arithmetic," Marco said. "How's your geography?"

"Ask me a question."

"What sea is Venice on?"

"I know," Maffeo replied, "but it's hard to say. It's the A ... the Adri ... I can't pronounce it."

"Adriatic," Marco said. "Do you know what sea Genoa is on?"

"I can't remember."

"It's an even bigger word than Adriatic," Marco said. "Genoa is on the Mediterranean Sea."

The boys knew that Venice was at war with Genoa. The two cities were fighting over the right to trade with countries in the East. This trade made the merchants of Europe very rich.

Venice was a great trading center in the land we now call Italy. Marco was born there more than 700 years ago.

In those days traders put European goods on ships in Venice and sent them to ports on the eastern end of the Mediterranean Sea. From there they would go by land to faraway countries in the East. People there paid high prices for glass, iron, woolens and fine jewelry.

In return, the Eastern countries sent spices, ivory, rugs and gold to the

Mediterranean ports. The ships from Venice would bring these home.

The boys' father, Nicolo Polo, was a trader. He was away on a long business trip with Uncle Maffeo. Marco's brother was named after Uncle Maffeo.

Marco and Maffeo did not know where their father and their uncle had gone. It was hard to send letters in those days. The boys had heard nothing from them for several years.

While their father was away their mother had died. The boys now lived with another uncle in a big house in Venice.

Venice has canals for streets. Long before Marco and Maffeo were born some wild tribes from the North invaded Italy. They drove some of the people to a group of small islands in the Adriatic Sea. Here

the people felt safer from attack. The water would protect them. So they built a city and called it Venice.

They used water for streets and where there was no water they dug canals. They traveled about in boats called gondolas. Marco liked to ride in gondolas.

One day the uncle that Marco and Maffeo lived with took them down to the piers where big ships docked. They watched a warship come in. A sailor on board told them that the Venetian navy had defeated the Genoan navy.

This made Marco feel better about his father. "We can stop worrying, Maffeo," he said to his brother. "Now that Venice rules the seas, I'm sure Father will come home safely."

2
Marco's Father Comes Home

When Marco was fifteen, he and Maffeo had their own gondola. One Sunday they went to mass at St. Mark's church.

As they were paddling home Marco said, "When I get to be a man I'm going to go look for Father." The years had gone by and still the boys had not heard from him.

"Do you think you'll find him?" Maffeo asked.

"I'll find him," Marco said, "even if I have to go all the way to China!"

Just then they reached the landing at their uncle's house. The boys jumped out and started tying the gondola to a post.

"Where is China?" Maffeo asked.

"A long, long way to the east," Marco said. "It's about a million miles from Venice!"

"Stop exaggerating, Marco!" It was their uncle speaking. He had come up without them seeing him.

"Well, maybe it's not a million miles," Marco said. "But it's a long, long way."

"It certainly is," his uncle agreed. "And there's someone in the house who can tell you more about that. Come inside, boys. I have a big surprise."

When they entered the house a tall man strode quickly forward to greet them. He put one arm around each boy.

Marco did not remember what his

father looked like. But he was sure this stranger was his father. He could feel it inside.

There were tears in the man's eyes. He could hardly speak. "My sons!" he cried proudly.

"Oh, Father!" Marco shouted happily. "You're back!"

Maffeo stared at his father. He was too shy to say anything.

The man looked the boys up and down. "My!" he exclaimed. "You've grown so tall!"

"What did you expect us to do?" Marco asked with a grin. "Stay little boys the whole time you were away?"

His father laughed. Another man came into the room.

"This is your Uncle Maffeo," their father said.

After they had greeted Uncle Maffeo they started asking questions.

"We've been all the way to China," Uncle Maffeo said.

"Wasn't it a dangerous trip?" Marco asked.

"In some ways it was," his father said. "But the road to China is safer now than it has been for hundreds of years."

Their father told them that there was a great king in China named Kublai Khan. People called him the Khan.

Before Kublai became the Khan it was almost impossible for Europeans to go to China. They were killed by bandits on the way or by native tribes who hated Christians. There was often war going on in the countries they had to pass through. But the Khan now ruled much of the land between China and Europe,

15

and there was peace. The Khan tried to make the roads safe. He wanted to meet people from Europe. He thought he could learn a great deal from them.

"We met Kublai Khan," Marco's father said. "He is a great king."

"He gave us a message to take to the Pope," Uncle Maffeo said. "He wants the Pope to send him 100 missionaries to teach his people."

"But there's no pope now," Marco said.

"We heard that on the way home," his father said. "But when a new pope is elected head of the Catholic church, we'll give him the message. We promised to guide the missionaries to China."

"He asked us to bring him some holy oil from Jerusalem too," Uncle Maffeo said. "He has heard that the oil has magic powers."

"I wish you'd stay home," Marco said.

"We made a promise to the Khan," his father replied.

"Let me go to China with you," Marco cried.

"No, Marco. You're too young. It's a hard trip. Sometimes the road crosses scorching deserts. Other times it is blocked by snow. And there are still some bandits. I know you're big, but you're still only fifteen."

Marco was disappointed. But he didn't give up. He still hoped he could go.

The next day Marco's father showed him some of the precious stones he had brought from China. There were diamonds, rubies and emeralds.

When he saw these beautiful gems sparkling in the sunlight Marco wanted to go to China more than ever.

3
Off for China!

Marco's father hoped a new pope would be elected soon so that he could deliver the Khan's message. But the cardinals who voted could not agree on a pope.

Young Marco began to hope that by the time they did agree he would be old enough to go to China.

Two years passed. Still there was no pope.

One morning at breakfast Marco's father said, "Son, you're a man now. You're seventeen. I think you will be a big help on our trip to China."

Marco could hardly believe the words he had heard! He was going to China! "Thank you, Father!" he cried. "Has a new pope been elected?"

"No," his father said. "But your Uncle Maffeo and I have decided to go back to China anyway. The Khan will be angry if we wait too long. We can't bring the missionaries, but we can bring the holy oil. We'll stop in Jerusalem on our way."

Marco was certainly excited. He hated to leave his brother. But he knew that Maffeo was needed in Venice in the family business. Maffeo was good at arithmetic. He already kept records for the business.

It was several weeks before the Polos started on their trip. Marco spent much of his time getting ready. He practiced shooting with his crossbow.

He hoped he would not have to fight on the trip. But he remembered what his father had said about bandits. Marco wanted to be prepared for anything.

One day in 1271, Marco, his father and his Uncle Maffeo boarded a ship and sailed out to sea. Some warships went with them to protect them from pirates.

Marco stood on the deck of the ship and watched Venice slowly disappear. The last thing he saw was the gilded domes of St. Mark's church. They gleamed like fire in the sunshine. Marco wondered if he would ever see them again.

When they reached Acre, a port in the Holy Land, the Polos got off the ship. They went to see an old friend named Tedaldo who was a priest.

"Has a pope been elected yet?" Marco's father asked.

"Not yet," Tedaldo said sadly.

"Well," Nicolo Polo said, disappointed, "we'll go to Jerusalem for the holy oil."

It was just a short trip from Acre to Jerusalem. The Polos got the oil and then started for China.

They had gone only a short distance when they had a message from Tedaldo. He asked them to return to Acre at once. Tedaldo himself had been elected pope. He took the name of Gregory X.

When the Polos saw him they asked for 100 missionaries. But Gregory X could find only two who would go. However, he gave the Polos some letters and presents to take to the Khan. Once more the Polos started for China.

Their route lay through Armenia, a country that was between Acre and Persia. When they reached the border of

Armenia they heard bad news. Armenia had just been invaded by Saracens.

The Saracens and Christians were enemies. They had been fighting for many years for control of the Holy Land. The two missionaries were afraid they would be tortured if the Saracens captured them. So the two missionaries turned back.

But the Polos went on. They were not afraid. The Khan had given Marco's father a golden tablet. It told all the Khan's people to help the Polos on their trip.

The Polos were not in the Khan's lands yet, but they would be soon. The Khan was the most powerful ruler in the world. The Polos felt sure the golden tablet would protect them from harm.

4
Ships of the Desert

The Polos usually traveled in caravans. The caravans were made up of many travelers going the same way. There was safety in numbers.

Some of the travelers rode on horses or mules. Others rode on camels. Marco was fascinated by the camels.

"These are Arabian camels," Uncle Maffeo told him. "They have just one hump. They are the kind used in most caravans. In Tibet you'll see another camel, the Bactrian camel. It has two humps."

Uncle Maffeo bought some camels to carry their supplies. But he insisted that they all ride horseback. "Camels are dangerous if you don't know how to handle them," he told Marco. "Sometimes they fly into terrible rages. They try to bite and kick the person nearest them."

But Marco learned to admire the camels. The big animals seldom got tired. And they could go for days without food or water.

"Camels mean everything to the people in this country," Marco said to his father. "The people drink their milk. They make clothes from camels' hair. And they sleep in camels' hair tents!"

The caravan came to a great stretch of sand. "Now you'll learn why camels are called ships of the desert," Marco's father told him. "They can cross a sea of sand just as easily as ships cross a sea of water. They can go 25 miles in one day with 1000 pounds on their backs!"

The caravan rested at the desert's edge. "There is almost nothing to eat or drink in the desert," a camel driver told Marco. "So we feed the animals more than they need before we start out. We give them a lot to drink too. Then they can travel for several days without food or water."

The camel driver talked on. "Camels are suited for living in deserts in other ways too. Their feet spread out so they don't sink in the sand. They have extra eyelids and can see in sandstorms that would blind men."

It was terribly hot in the desert. The sun blazed down from a cloudless sky. Marco hated the burning sands. But the heat did not seem to bother the camels.

When they reached the other side of the desert they camped in a group of date palm trees. They ate dates for supper.

The next morning there was a surprise for Marco. A baby had been born to one of the camels. It was three feet tall. But it was so weak it could hardly walk.

A camel driver put the baby in a hammock on one side of a big freight camel.

"Why don't you put the baby on the mother's back?" Marco asked.

"Because camels are so stupid," the driver said. "If I put the baby on the mother's back, the mother couldn't see it. A mother camel won't travel unless she can watch her baby. But now she will follow the camel that carries the baby."

Marco became fond of the baby camel

and helped take care of it. But not for long.

The caravan came to a dusty plain. That night the travelers slept under the stars. Marco was awakened suddenly by the sound of horses galloping.

"Bandits!" his father cried. "Get up, Marco!"

"Let's go!" Uncle Maffeo shouted.

The three Polos leaped on their horses and raced into the darkness. They heard screams and the noise of fighting behind them.

They also heard the sounds of bandits riding after them. An arrow whizzed by Marco's ear. He leaned over and begged his horse to run faster.

The Polos saw a town ahead, its walls bathed in moonlight. The bandits were now only a few yards behind. The horse

Uncle Maffeo was riding was hit by an arrow, but the horse raced on. Just in time the Polos reached the gates of the town and dashed through to safety.

The bandits left and after a time the Polos started out once more. Later, they learned that many members of the caravan had been killed. Others had been sold as slaves. Marco never saw the baby camel again.

5

A Tower of Gold

One night the Polos were sitting around their campfire talking.

"Young man," Marco's father said to him, "keep your eyes open on this trip. Try to remember everything you see. Kublai Khan will want to hear all about our trip."

"Oh, I already have a million things to tell him," Marco bragged.

"There you go exaggerating again," his father smiled. "The Khan likes stories too. So try to remember any good stories you hear."

Marco made notes about the things he saw. He described the trees, the animals and the way the people lived.

They came to a big city and decided to stay for several weeks. Marco was quick at learning languages. It wasn't long before he could talk to the people.

One night he told his father that he had a good story for the Khan.

"Let me hear it," his father said.

"Years ago there was a rich chief who lived near here in Bagdad. He was so rich that he had a tower filled with millions of pieces of gold. But he would not spend any of it."

"He was a thrifty man," Marco's father said.

"Let me finish, Father. He was a stupid man. He was so mean and miserly that he would not pay for a strong army. He

didn't have nearly enough soldiers to defend Bagdad. Even so, he got into a war with a prince from another country.

"The prince attacked Bagdad. He captured the chief. When the prince saw all the gold in the tower he was amazed.

" 'Chief,' the prince asked, 'why didn't you use your gold to pay for a strong army? If you had I couldn't have captured you.'

"At first the chief did not reply.

" 'What good is your gold now?' the prince asked.

" 'I love my gold!' the chief cried. 'Please don't take it away.'

" 'All right,' the prince said, 'you can keep your gold. But gold is all you can have. You can eat your gold. You can drink your gold. But you can eat and drink nothing else.'

"The prince locked the chief up in his tower. Of course, the chief couldn't eat gold. So he soon died of hunger and thirst.

"Isn't that a good story, Father?"

"Very good," Marco's father said. "It proves that it is evil to love money too much. I'm sure the Khan will like that story."

6

China at Last!

Marco woke up one morning feeling sick. He had a high fever.

"We must stay in this village until Marco gets well," his father said. Weeks and months went by, but Marco did not get well.

One night Marco was tossing in his sleep. He was having bad nightmares. Suddenly he woke up and heard low voices.

"Marco doesn't seem to be getting any better," he heard his father say. "I'm terribly worried about him."

"So am I," Uncle Maffeo said. "I'm worried about all three of us. We promised the Khan we'd be in China long ago. I'm afraid he may be angry when we do get there."

Marco went back to sleep. He dreamed that the Khan, waving a silver sword, was chasing him.

The next morning Uncle Maffeo said, "I've just heard about a place near here where sick people get well. It's up in the hills where the air is cool and clean. Let's take Marco there."

They set out the next day. Marco was very weak. He could hardly stay on his horse.

The higher they traveled into the hills, the more beautiful it became. Marco began to feel a little better when they reached the forests and the clear

mountain streams. After a few days in the cool, fresh air, Marco was well enough to continue the trip to China.

The Polos went on up into some huge mountains. It was hard work climbing the rocky trails. When they came out of the mountains they entered Lop, a city on the edge of a great desert. Today we call it the Gobi Desert.

"The trip across the desert takes a whole month," Marco's father said. "We must rest here before we start out."

Marco did not rest much. He bought some camels for the trip. These were Bactrian camels with two humps.

One night Uncle Maffeo said, "A caravan is starting across the desert tomorrow morning. We shall join it."

"I'll stay up late and load our camels," Marco said.

The next morning when they started across the desert Marco was tired. The sun shining on the sand hurt his eyes.

"We will come to an oasis late tonight," his father said. "We will find water there."

"We must be sure to *reach* the oasis," Uncle Maffeo said. "I've heard that terrible things happen in this desert."

Long before it got dark Marco became sleepy. The rocking motion of his horse made it hard for him to stay awake. After the sun went down he could not keep his eyes open. He went to sleep sitting on his horse.

The horse seemed to know that Marco was asleep. He went slower and slower until finally he and Marco were far behind the caravan. They were alone in the great desert.

An hour later Marco woke up. He could not see the caravan. He could not even see the tracks of the other animals. The wind had covered the tracks with sand. Marco was frightened. He had no water with him. If he did not find the caravan he would die of thirst.

Suddenly he thought he heard voices. "Marco! Marco!" they seemed to say. "Come this way, Marco!"

"Ah!" Marco thought with relief. "That's Father and Uncle Maffeo. I'll catch up with them in a few minutes."

He turned his horse north in the direction of the voices. He rode as fast as he could. But he couldn't find the caravan. The voices always seemed to be a short distance ahead. Shortly before dawn he stopped hearing the voices.

The sun rose in the east. The air

became hotter and hotter. Marco became terribly thirsty. He would have to find the caravan soon or he would die.

Marco looked in every direction. But there was only a sea of sand.

"The caravan was traveling to the east," he said to himself. "I turned my horse north when I woke up. That means the caravan must be east and south of here. The sun rises in the east. If I head a little south of the sun I should find the caravan."

Marco rode for hours. Once he stopped and put a pebble under his tongue. He had heard that a pebble would help cure thirst. But it didn't help much.

Marco was about ready to give up hope. Just then some shapes appeared above the heat waves dancing over the sand. Trees! It was an oasis. As Marco came closer he saw that the caravan was camped near the trees.

There was a well at the oasis. Marco drank slowly. Water had never tasted so good.

"Don't ever fall asleep on a horse again," Marco's father said.

"I thought I heard you calling," Marco explained. "I followed the voices and got lost."

Of course, Marco had not heard real voices. Scientists now know that desert sands make sounds when they cool off at night. Marco thought the sounds were the voices of his father and Uncle Maffeo.

All three Polos were careful during the rest of the trip. They reached the other side of the desert safely. They had been traveling more than three years. But now they were in China at last!

7

Kublai Khan

The Polos learned that Kublai Khan was at his summer palace at Xanadu. It was a 40-day trip. The roads were good and there were comfortable houses for travelers along the way.

Several miles before they reached Xanadu they could see the Khan's palace standing high on a hill. It was a huge building made of gleaming marble.

While Marco gazed in wonder a group of horsemen in uniform dashed out of the palace gates. They galloped up to the Polos and escorted them to the palace.

The palace doors swung open and the Polos stepped inside. The walls were colored gold. There were many pictures of wild animals and birds, flowers, dragons and soldiers at war. Marco had never seen such a dazzling sight.

The Polos were led to a long hall. At the far end they saw Kublai Khan sitting on his throne. He was wearing robes of silk decorated with green dragons.

Suddenly, Marco became worried. What if the Khan did not welcome them. Suppose he was angry because they had spent so much time on the trip.

When they were a few yards from the throne the Polos threw themselves on the floor. This was the way the people in China showed their respect to the Khan.

"Stand up!" the Khan ordered in a thundering voice.

The Polos stood up. There was a moment of silence. Then in a hearty tone the Khan said, "Welcome to China!"

The Khan did not seem to notice Marco. But it was clear that he was glad to see Marco's father and uncle. He had become fond of them when they were in China before.

Marco's father gave the Khan the holy oil and presents from the Pope. The Khan thanked him.

Then he looked at Marco for the first time. His black eyes seemed to bore right through him. "Who is this young man?" he asked, pointing a finger at Marco.

"That is your servant," Marco's father said, *"and my son."*

The Khan smiled. *"He is welcome and it pleases me much."*

Marco breathed easier.

That night the Khan gave a big party for the Polos. For the first time in his life Marco ate from plates made of gold. And he drank from golden goblets.

The next morning Kublai Khan sent for Marco. "Tell me about your trip," he said. Marco didn't know it, but the Khan was testing him.

Marco described the long trip from Venice. Then he told the Khan about the chief who starved to death in the tower full of gold.

"You know how to tell a good story," the Khan said.

The Khan thought for a moment. "Marco," he went on, "I have a job for a man who can keep his eyes and ears open. I need a man I can trust to tell the truth. How would you like to work for me?"

"I'd like it, sir!" Marco cried.

"It would be an important job," the Khan continued. "You would travel about my great empire and find out what goes on in the different places. Sometimes your life might be in danger. I have many enemies as well as friends. What's more, there are many wild beasts in the forests. Sometimes they attack travelers."

"I'm not afraid of wild animals," Marco bragged.

"Are you sure?" the Khan asked.

The Khan gave three short whistles. Then he pointed to the door. Marco looked and his heart froze in his throat. An enormous lion was coming through the door.

Now Marco realized the Khan was testing him. If he ran he knew the Khan would not give him the job.

The lion walked slowly toward Marco and the Khan. When he was a few feet away he opened his mouth and bared his deadly fangs. Marco was terrified. But he stood his ground.

Slowly the lion closed his mouth. Then he lay down on the floor at the feet of the Khan and went to sleep.

The Khan reached over and patted the lion's back. "He's tame, Marco. He's my pet. But most people don't know he's tame. They think that when he lies down at my feet he's showing respect for me. A lion may be king of the jungle. But I'm the greatest king on earth. That's what I want my people to think."

Marco laughed.

"Were you afraid?" the Khan asked.

"Yes," Marco said truthfully.

"Yet you didn't try to run," the Khan

said. "You are a brave young man. I need a brave man to work for me. Do you still want the job?"

"Yes, yes!" Marco cried.

"You will have to talk to many people. My people speak several languages. Do you think you can learn their languages?"

"I know I can," Marco said. "I learned to speak *your* language on my way here."

"Good," the Khan said. "Start learning the languages at once."

8

Rivers of Gold

When the Khan moved to his winter palace at Cambaluc, the Polos went with him. Marco was busy studying languages. His father and Uncle Maffeo were busy trading. Cambaluc was a rich city and a great trading center.

"Rare things from many parts of Asia find their way to Cambaluc," Uncle Maffeo told Marco. "A thousand pack horses loaded with silk enter the city each day."

Marco liked to wander through the noisy market place and look at the colorful things laid out for sale. There were spices, drugs, cloth of gold, precious stones, ivory and rugs. Marco was interested in the paper money the traders used. Paper money was unknown in Venice.

However, Marco did not have time for many trips to the market place. His studies took most of his time.

One day the Khan sent for Marco. "I hear you have learned your languages well," the Khan said.

"I have studied hard," Marco said.

"Good!" the Khan cried. "I have an important job for you. I want you to explore Karazan. Find out what it is like and report back to me."

Marco was gone a long time. When he

returned to Cambaluc he went straight to the Khan.

"Tell me about Karazan," the Khan ordered.

"There is gold in the rivers," Marco said, "and there is gold in the mountains."

"Fine!" the Khan cried. "I'm glad my country is so rich. Did you see any strange animals in Karazan?"

"I was almost eaten up by one," Marco said. "Once I was exploring a swampy place. I saw what I thought was a log and I stepped on it."

"What was it?" the Khan asked.

"It certainly wasn't a log," Marco said. "It moved when I stepped on it. I jumped as far away as I could. When I looked back I saw that my 'log' was a huge serpent with short legs. The serpent snapped at me. Its jaws were big enough

to swallow a man. Its teeth were large and sharp as knives. I got away from there as quickly as I could."

Marco had stepped on a crocodile.

As Marco grew older the Khan trusted him more. He sent him on many trips to far places—to India and Burma.

Once the Khan sent Marco to a place where most of the villages had been destroyed in a war. Marco and his guide had to camp out at night.

One afternoon they pitched their tent by a bamboo thicket. When it got dark they built a fire and started supper.

In the distance they heard a tiger scream. Another tiger called back.

"Quick!" the guide said. "We must scare them away. Help me cut some bamboo canes."

Marco wondered what good the bamboo

would do. The tiger's screams came closer and closer.

"Hurry!" the guide shouted. "Throw the canes on the fire."

Marco almost smothered the fire with the bamboo. A bloodthirsty howl only a few yards away told him the beasts were ready to attack.

Just then a loud explosion came from the campfire. It was followed by a whole series of bangs and pops. "Bang! Pop! BANG!"

The loud noises scared the savage tigers. They fled in terror.

Marco learned that bamboo canes are hollow inside. As the canes burned the air in the hollow spaces expanded. It made the canes explode.

After that Marco always cut some bamboo canes before he made his fire.

9

Surprise Attack!

Kublai Khan had a relative named Nayan who was in command of one of the Khan's armies. This army was stationed a long way from Cambaluc.

Nayan was much younger than the Khan and he thought he was smarter. He wanted to be the Khan.

So he made secret plans to overthrow Kublai. He knew that the Khan had a nephew named Kaidu. Kaidu was also head of a powerful army. Nayan knew that Kaidu hated his uncle. He asked Kaidu to help wage war on the Khan.

Together they should be strong enough to defeat the Khan's army.

Kaidu agreed. The two men tried to keep their plans secret. They wanted to make a surprise attack. If they struck before the Khan's army was ready, they were sure they would win.

But one of the Khan's spies heard of their plans. And the Khan told Marco.

"What are you going to do?" Marco asked.

"I'll attack first," the Khan said. "I'll attack Nayan before Kaidu's army joins him. My army will be stronger than his is alone."

The Khan didn't usually travel with his army. He left the fighting to his soldiers. But this time he decided to go. He took Marco with him.

They set out with the army. After

many days they came to some high hills. Scouts told them that Nayan's army was camped on the other side.

The Khan halted his troops. He told them to rest for two days. He sent scouts ahead. They were to capture Nayan's scouts. The Khan wanted to be sure to surprise Nayan.

While the Khan's army rested the soldiers talked about the coming battle. Some of them were afraid.

The Khan had some men with him who thought they could tell the future by looking at the stars. These men were astrologers. The Khan asked the astrologers which side would win the battle. The astrologers studied the stars and then reported to the Khan.

The Khan called his army together. He turned to one of the astrologers and in a loud voice asked, "Who will win the battle?"

One of the astrologers stepped forward. "The stars say you will win, my lord."

A mighty roar arose from the soldiers. They were not afraid now.

Early the next morning the Khan's army started climbing the hills. Some soldiers were on foot. Others rode horses.

Marco rode with the Khan in a fort built on the backs of four elephants. Many archers rode in the Khan's fort too. The elephants wore armor made of thick leather, hardened by fire.

The fort was decorated with brilliant colored silks. The Khan's flag, with a picture of the sun and the moon, flew above it.

At last the Khan's army reached the top of the hills overlooking a great plain.

Spread over the plain were the tents of the army of Nayan. The Khan had taken Nayan completely by surprise!

The Khan's army rushed into Nayan's camp. Nayan was asleep in his tent. The noise of the fighting awakened him, and he ran out to lead his soldiers.

It was a fierce and bloody battle. The men fought with crossbows, lances and swords.

"The air was filled with a cloud of arrows," Marco said later. "They poured down on every side. Many men and horses fell to the ground. The loud cries and shouts of the men and the noise of the horses and weapons filled everyone with terror."

The battle raged all through the morning. Bodies of men and horses were piled high on the field.

Finally, Nayan's army began to retreat in defeat. Nayan and all his officers were captured and brought before the Khan.

The Khan ordered that Nayan, the traitor, be put to death. But Nayan was a relative of the Khan. A man of royal blood could not be killed in front of an army of common people.

So Nayan was hidden between two carpets. Then a group of the Khan's soldiers grabbed the carpets at both ends. They shook Nayan up and down as hard as they could. He was shaken to death.

Nayan's soldiers swore to be loyal to the Khan. When Kaidu heard that the Khan had won he was afraid to fight him alone. The Khan had no more trouble with him.

10

Dreams of Home

The three Polos had now been in China for many years. It is probable that Marco had traveled more than any other man in the world up to that time.

And his father and uncle had made a fortune. Their trading business was a great success.

The Khan had been good to them all. But he was now an old man. He could not live much longer. The Polos wanted to leave China before he died.

They were afraid that the next Khan might not treat them so well. He might even kill them. Many people in China were jealous of the Polos.

At first the Polos were afraid to ask if they could leave. They knew the Khan liked Marco's work. It would be hard for him to find someone else to do Marco's job.

One day Marco's father noticed that the Khan was in a good humor. He thought this was the time to ask for a favor.

"Great Khan," he said, "we would like to go back to our home in Venice."

"What!" cried Kublai Khan. "After all I have done for you!"

"Maffeo and I are getting old," Nicolo Polo argued. "We want to see our people again. And Marco is almost 40. He wants to marry and settle down."

"It's a dangerous trip!" the Khan shouted. "You might lose your lives on the way."

"We know that," Nicolo said. "But my brother and I have made the trip safely two times."

Still the Khan refused. He offered the Polos more riches than they had. He offered them honors. But he would not let them leave.

"I need Marco," he said. Marco's father and uncle would not go without him.

Marco was disappointed that he could not return to Venice. But an exciting trip was in store for him just the same. The Khan sent him south to Indochina and the Spice Islands. The spices that the Europeans liked so much grew in these islands.

Marco was in command of one of the

ships. He had sailed for the Khan before. He knew more about sailing than many men in China.

While Marco was away, three Persian ambassadors came to see the Khan. They were sent by their King whose name was Argun.

The ambassadors told the Khan that their king's wife had died. Before she died she made Argun promise that he would marry a woman from her family. Her family lived in China. The ambassadors asked the Khan to help them find a new queen among his people.

The Khan found a beautiful princess named Kogatin. She was seventeen.

The ambassadors started for Persia with Kogatin. But they had to turn back. A war had broken out and the way was blocked.

So they returned to Cambaluc. There they met Marco's father and uncle. And soon they met Marco himself, back from his long voyage.

The ambassadors learned that the Polos wanted to return to Venice. They knew that Persia was on the way to Venice. They also knew that Marco was a good sailor. So the ambassadors went to see the Khan again.

"We cannot go to Persia by land," one of them said. "So we want your permission to go by sea."

"You may go," the Khan said.

"But sir," the ambassador cried, "we know nothing about sailing. Won't you let the Polos go with us? Marco knows the seas we must travel."

The Khan frowned. He did not want to let Marco go. But he had promised

to send a new queen to Persia. He said
he would think it over.

Finally he sent for the Polos. "I have
decided to let you go home," he said.
"But before you go I want you to make
me a promise.

"What is it, sir?" Marco asked.

"Promise that you'll come back," the
Khan said, "after you have stayed a
while in Venice."

The Polos promised that they would return to China. Then the Khan gave them two golden tablets. They were like the ones he had given Marco's father so many years before.

"These golden tablets," the Khan said, "will take you safely through my lands. Show them to my people and they will give you all the food, supplies and help that you need."

The Polos thanked the Khan. Now they must decide how to take their riches home. Chinese paper money would have no value in Venice. Gold was too heavy to carry in large amounts. So the Polos used their riches to buy diamonds, rubies, emeralds, sapphires and pearls.

The Polos ripped open the seams of some of their clothes. They sewed the jewels in the seams. Now they need not worry if they met robbers on the trip. The precious stones were safely hidden.

11

"Marco Million"

The Khan gave the Polos and the Princess fourteen ships for the trip, and supplies for two years. Many people traveled with them.

After a voyage of more than two years the ships reached Persia. There was sad news for the Princess. While they had been at sea King Argun had died.

At first the Polos did not know what to do with Kogatin. Then they took her to meet Argun's son, Kasan. Kasan liked the Princess. He decided to marry her. Kogatin would be a queen after all.

The Polos were still a long way from their home in Venice. They continued their trip westward over the deserts of Persia. One day they heard more sad news. The great Kublai Khan was dead.

This meant that they did not have to keep their promise to return to China. Now that the Khan was dead the roads might even be closed.

At last the Polos reached the Mediterranean Sea. They boarded a ship and sailed on toward home. When the ship reached the Adriatic Sea it turned toward Venice.

As they neared the city they could see the gilded domes of St. Mark's church rising in the sky. Tears filled Marco's eyes. He was home at last. They had been away for 24 years!

Marco was now 41 years of age. His

face was suntanned and weather-beaten. He had a beard. His father and uncle had white hair now.

"Do you think anyone in Venice will remember us?" Marco asked his father.

"I think so," his father said.

But his father was wrong. When the Polos landed in Venice they were wearing their traveling clothes. They were shabby from the long trip. The Polos looked poor and unimportant. The fancy clothes from China were still in their trunks.

A man on the dock eyed Marco scornfully. "Who are you?"

"We are the Polos of Venice."

"You are a liar," the man cried. "The Polos are dead."

Marco laughed at that. "Where is my brother?" he asked.

"I don't think you have a brother," the

man said. "But if you mean Maffeo Polo he won't help you. He's not in Venice."

That was a blow. Surely his brother would have remembered them.

Then Marco got a bright idea. He decided they should have a big party. He invited many important people to come. The people did not believe they were the Polos. But they accepted out of curiosity.

Before the party the Polos unpacked their trunks. When their guests arrived the Polos were wearing expensive clothes made of Chinese silk. Their jackets glittered with golden decorations.

The guests had never seen such beautiful clothes. After they had admired the clothes the Polos took them off. Marco threw them to the servants.

"Cut them up," Marco said. "Divide the silk among yourselves."

Then the Polos dressed again. Their clothes were even more gorgeous than before. Their silken jackets were decorated with green dragons.

Again they gave their clothes to the servants to keep. The guests were beginning to believe they must be rich men if they could give away such valuable silks.

Finally, Marco brought out the shabby

clothes that they had worn when they arrived in Venice.

"These are the most valuable clothes of all," Marco said with a laugh.

"They don't look valuable to me," one of the guests said.

"Just wait," Marco said. He got a knife and opened the seams. Hundreds of rubies, emeralds, diamonds, sapphires and pearls fell upon the floor. The precious

jewels sparkled in the light of the candles on the table.

"Now will you believe we are the Polos?" Marco asked. "Only men who have been to China could bring back such riches."

"Yes! Yes! I believe you now!" a guest shouted. The others joined in.

"We're glad you've come home," a leading citizen said. "Welcome back to Venice."

The Polos settled down and enjoyed their wealth. Marco liked to talk about his travels. He bragged about the millions of people who lived in China and the millions of sights he had seen.

He used the word "million" so much that his friends gave him a nickname. They called him "Marco Million."

12

"Father of Geography"

A few years after Marco returned to Venice he had to leave again. This time it was to go to war with Genoa.

Marco was the commander of a Venetian warship. During a fierce battle with the fleet from Genoa, his ship was captured. Marco was taken to Genoa and thrown in prison.

Prison life was boring. The prisoners had little to do to pass the long hours, so Marco entertained them with tales of his travels. Even the jail guards enjoyed Marco's stories.

One of Marco's prison friends was named Rusticiano. "Your stories about your travels are interesting, Marco," Rusticiano said. "Why don't you write a book about them?"

"I haven't the patience to write a book," Marco said.

"You don't have to write it," Rusticiano said. "I will. You tell me what to write."

Marco thought that was a good idea. He and Rusticiano worked for many long hours on the book. They named it *The Travels of Marco Polo.*

There were no printing presses in Europe when Marco was alive. But many men copied his book by hand. They passed it from one person to another. Many people read it.

Soon after the book was finished Marco was let out of prison. He went back to

Venice where he married and had three daughters. He died in about 1324.

But Marco's book lived on and on. Map-makers used it and so did explorers. Even today many scholars study Marco's book.

The book tells about his travels and the many strange things he saw. It also describes some places that he did not see, but heard about, such as Japan.

Other men from Europe had been to Asia. But no one wrote about it the way Marco did. No one described things in such careful detail.

After Kublai Khan died all of the land routes to China were closed. No Europeans could go to China, India or the Spice Islands.

But men dreamed of finding a new way to the rich lands described by Marco.

More than 175 years after Marco wrote his book Christopher Columbus read it. The book gave Columbus an idea.

"If the land route to Asia is closed," he thought, "why not try the sea?" There is a copy of Marco's book in Spain with notes written in it by Columbus.

It was while looking for China, India, Japan and the Spice Islands that Columbus discovered America. If Marco Polo had not written his book America might not have been discovered until much later.

Many people did not believe Marco Polo. However, geographers today know that the descriptions in his book were amazingly accurate. The book helped make geography a real science. That is why Marco Polo is often called "the Father of Geography."